An
Anishinaabe
Native American
Pow wow

Authorized by

Chief Jim Wilson
Nuluti Equani Ehi Tribe
Yadkin County, North Carolina

An *Anishinaabe* Native American Pow wow © 2014.
All rights reserved by the Nuluti Equani Ehi Tribe,
Jim Wilson, Principle Chief

W & B Publishers

For information:
W & B Publishers
Post Office Box 193
Colfax, NC 27235
www.a-argusbooks.com

ISBN: 978-1-4949637-8-1
ISBN: 1-4949637-8-7

Book Cover designed by Dubya

Printed in the United States of America

State of North Carolina

PAT McCRORY

GOVERNOR

NULUTI EQUANI EHI TRIBE NATIVE AMERICAN WEEKEND

2013

BY THE GOVERNOR OF THE STATE OF NORTH CAROLINA

A PROCLAMATION

WHEREAS, the 2013 Strong Sun Pow Wow marks the 260th Anniversary of the White Feather Treaty of 1753; and

WHEREAS, the White Feather Treaty solidified friendship and cultural understanding between the ancestors of the Nuluti Equani Ehi Tribe and settlers in Bethabara, Wachovia, Bethania, Clemmons, Yadkinville, East Bend and areas in Wilkes, Surry, Stokes, Davidson and Iredell Counties, for the purpose of protection, friendship and growth; and

WHEREAS, the White Feather Treaty also promoted peace, unity and pride in cultural heritage for all people, and provided a foundation for future generations of the region to build upon; and

WHEREAS, the State of North Carolina joins the Nuluti Equani Ehi Tribe of Forsyth and Yadkin Counties in celebrating 260 years of friendship at the 2013 Strong Sun Pow Wow;

NOW, THEREFORE, I, Pat McCrory, Governor of the State of North Carolina, do hereby proclaim July 12-14, 2013, in recognition of **"NULUTI EQUANI EHI TRIBE NATIVE AMERICAN WEEKEND"** in North Carolina, and commend its observance to all citizens.

IN WITNESS WHEREOF, I have hereunto set my hand and affixed the Great Seal of the State of North Carolina at the Capitol in Raleigh this eighth day of July in the year of our Lord two thousand and thirteen, and of the Independence of the United States of America the two hundred and thirty-eighth.

PAT McCRORY

Governor

Proclamation of Native American Weekend, N.C. Governor Pat McCrory,

NULUTI EQUNI EHI (Near River Dwellers)

Yadkin Valley, North Carolina

Who we are

Tribal History 1752 - 2013

The title Nuluti Equani Ehi is Cherokee and, loosely translated, identifies the our tribe as Near River Dwellers. Our history goes back to Jamestown and even further, as far back as our original home in Canada. We, like many other Anishinaabe tribes, are of Algonquin decent as well as sharing mixed blood with the Delaware, the Cherokee and many other tribes and nation, in which some of our bloodline descendents are very active in their current leadership.

As the invading settlers expanded and wrested territory from our people, the tribe was forced to move further into Virginia, West Virginia and other areas, including much of what is now the Yadkin River Valley area of North Carolina. According to our native customs, we have always been farmers living on the rivers to utilize the proximity of nearby water for irrigation as well as a source of food. Some of the many rivers inhabited by our ancestors were the Delaware River, James River, New River, Dan River and the Yadkin River and our tribe stretches as far south as the Gulf of Mexico. History and genealogy, as well as recorded history and our own oral history passed down from generation to generation, support this fact.

During our history, there has been a lot of marriages between various tribes, as well as marriage between the Native Americans and the settlers. For the settlers, it was a way to increase wealth. For the Native Americans, it was a way to avoid war and increase trade capabilities.

Prior to the settlement of Bethabara in 1753, our ancestors lived along the Yadkin River. Movement along the Yadkin was accomplished by rafts and crude canoes made by members of the tribe, however, much of the travel was on foot following alongside the river banks. The continued migration lead to inter-marriage into many tribes on the rivers, one such movement being arrival at the Saura villages, resulting in inter-marrying with the Saura. By the mid 1700's, the Saura people had gone into hiding or had merged with other tribes in order to survive and hopefully prosper. Our tribal ancestry in these areas dates to and before the presence of a chief known in the white language as Chief Donnaha. This title is a point of interest and quite a lot of confusion, as there were several Chief Donnaha's. "Donnaha" is actually a Saura title, not a name and is also the English way of addressing the Chief of the area as his full title was too hard for the English settlers to pronounce. Adding to the confusion, there were at this time two tribes that were so identical in dress, language, customs and mannerisms. the only way to tell the difference between members of the two tribes was the way they wore their hair.

There is much more about our history that we share at talks, crafting classes, gatherings and Pow Wow's. If you feel you may be a part of our history or wish to learn more, please contact our office to arrange a lecture or a book signing. If you are seeking a tribal home, we would be honored to talk with you. Visit us at our website: http://nearriverdwellers.com

Declaration of Sovereignty
Of the
Nuluti Equani Ehi Tribe

We the people; of the Nuluti Equani Ehi Tribe; being descended from many separate Native American Tribes, Bands, Nations. Do together join with the men, women and children of all Nations in standing before the threshold of time.

We acknowledge our desire for this document, and the actions of our leaders and our people to stand as a beacon of hope unto any man, woman or child who is of Native American decent, and whose family or who themselves may have been denied admission into the limited tribal roles which were acknowledged and established by the conquering government of the United States: We recognize that their role was not written to truly be a record of all the descendants of the indigenous tribes of the United States, but were rather to establish and limit the degree of their responsibility unto such person both then and in the future; and considering that the objective of methods was to annihilate any Tribe or any people, who by their own standards "had no written language or constitution and to erase all memories of them and their people from the face of the earth forever, We feel compelled by the spirit of grace, to open the doors of admission into our tribe unto any man, woman or child who can demonstrate that they have even one Indian descendant in their line of ancestors, and in so doing, to afford these descendants of this unspeakable tragedy the opportunity to reestablish at least some remembrance of their people, and the ways of their people; among and with, other indigenous people, who themselves strive to establish the same thing; and in unity to combine our knowledge, our strength, our hope, our education, and our resources, to secure for ourselves and our prosperity justice, peace, and liberty which with the blessing of the creator may afford the opportunity to not only set right one of the worst tragedies in the history of this world, but also to live as a nation within a nation, and in peace among those, who in the age of their own ignorance and having the eyes of their understanding darkened and blinded to the true outcome of their deeds, did engage in and create this holocaust; and together to strive to build such a future, that all future generations as long as the Sun shall shine, and the Moon gives it's light, many witness our actions this day and the deeds of those who help us in this endeavor to stand as a testimony of the healing grace of our creator, and prove to be a blessing for both our people, and theirs as well, and our prayer before creating these things is that many may prove to be the memorial unto our fallen that shall enable their memories and their names be remembered and to stand forever thought-out all the generations; and that this will become the flame of the fire of desire that will burn in the hearts of our people today and thought-out the ages Amen.

The Pow Wow

The Pow Wow is a celebration of traditions, the earliest of which—according to modern records—was around 1877. It was a celebration after the removal of the Indian to Indian Territory. A celebration of arrival after the hardships of the journey and so many had died along the road to Oklahoma. The word "pow wow" derives from our ancestors and is an Algonquin term for a gathering of medicine men and spiritual leaders in a curing ceremony, "pauau" or "pau wau." Historically, even before records were kept, all tribes held ceremonies or get-togethers to celebrate gatherings (our family reunion), warfare, sing, dance, visit and feast. These ceremonies allowed people to give thanks, honor their deceased relatives, or give special honors, such as name-giving ceremonies and coming-of-age rite. Many times they were held to renew allegiances and maintain friendships with members of visiting tribes.

During the Pow Wow, wisdom passes from the elders to the children, the most important asset of Native American people. The young, who are just beginning their journey through life, and the elders. who are nearing the completion of their journey, share closeness to the Creator.

Welcome to the
Nuluti Equani Ehi Tribe
Pow-Wow

Before describing the Nuluti Equani Ehi Tribe Pow-Wow, we must inform all that there exists thousands of Native American tribes in the United States and even more in Canada, Mexico, Central and South America. All of those tribes have their own method of conducting a Pow-Wow and the traditions of one tribe is most likely considerably different than the traditions of another. A northern tribe will conduct its ceremonies different than a southern tribe. The Cherokee will be different from the Catawba; the Lakota different than the Pueblo. There is no one perfect method, yet every Pow-Wow pays honor to the Great Spirit, our Creator.

This is the Pow Wow of the Nuluti Equani Ehi Tribe and the ceremonies described and pictured herein are our ceremonies—our fashion of showing our love and respect to our Creator and to Mother Earth.

*****

At the beginning of an Nuluti Equani Ehi Tribe Pow wow, certain honored warriors of the tribe identified as "Grass Dancers" perform the ritual *Grass Dance.* In ages past, it was often necessary that tall grass be flattened in order that the other dancers could perform without tripping. As the tradition grew, the Grass Dancers were charged with the blessing of the grounds. Although it is seldom necessary to flatten grass in modern times, the blessing of the grounds is still a time-honored tradition performed before the Pow-Wow can begin.

Native American Grass Dancers

Native American Grass Dancers

Once the Grass Dance has been completed the Pow-Wow is officially ready to begin. The spokesman known as the Arena Director sounds the call for the "Grand Entry." All of the participants line up in single file for the Grand Entry procession that begins at the East Gate.

North

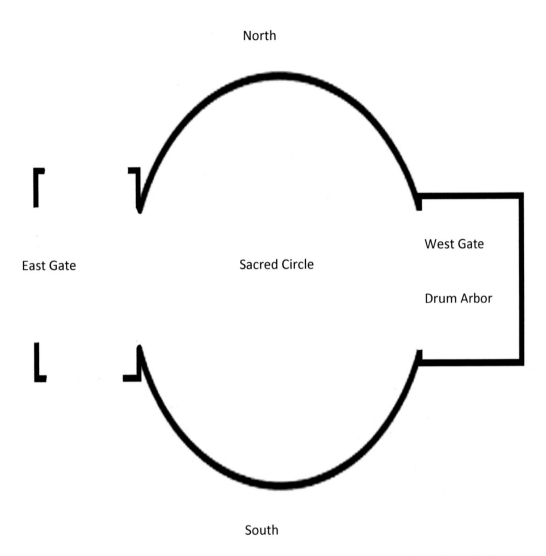

East Gate   Sacred Circle   West Gate

                                              Drum Arbor

South

On the opposite side of the circle is the West Gate, which is where the tribal drum is located in the Drum Arbor. The "West Gate" is not an entrance gate, rather it is a tent that protects the tribal drum from the elements. Nothing begins until the drum beat begins.

*****

The Grand Entrance Procession

The Grand Entry signifies the beginning of the Pow wow.

The procession is headed by the tribal Chief, or by a designated dignitary. That person caries the Eagle Staff. At times, there may be more than one Eagle Staff, and if so, the other Eagle Staff bearers follow behind the Chief.

Immediately in line behind the Eagle Staff bearers comes the individual designated to carry the Stars and Stripes flag of the United States of America.

Next in line comes the Veterans of the U .S. Armed Forces to whom honor is paid. These veterans may be carrying flags from their individual unit or from their particular branch of service flag. Someone, normally one of the veterans who is likely a Native American, may be designated to carry the Missing in Action Flag, also known as the Prisoner of War Flag..

Another individual may be assigned the responsibility of carrying the State Flag, in our case the North Carolina flag, while others may carry flags of different tribes or nations.

Next in line comes the dancers, and what a sight it is to see the Native American people in full Regalia.

Nothing happens until the drum, which is the heartbeat of the People and of Mother Earth starts its beat.

The procession, in single file, passes through the East Gate, dancing to the beat of the drum and enters the circle. The procession line continues in a clockwise manner, symbolizing the movement of the sun. The procession continues in an ever-tightening spiral until every one of the participants are in the circle, with the flag bearers standing facing the West Gate. Then, on signal, each flag is planted into the ground in front of the Drum Arbor. The Eagle Staff or Staffs are planted first to the right—or north side of the West Gate, with other flags to the right of the Eagle Staff, and the United States Flag is placed on the right, or south side of the West Gate.

Throughout the Pow wow there are a series of dances, music and story-telling by members of the Nuluti Equani Ehi Tribe or by guests who may be from different tribes across the United States, Canada, Mexico as well as Central and South America.

One of the more recognizable of the Native American dances is the Hoop Dance.

The Hoop Dancer

During the dance, shapes are formed in story-telling ritual such as the butterfly, the eagle, the snake, and the coyote, with the hoop symbolizing the never-ending circle of life. The Hoop dance focuses on very rapid moves, and the construction of hoop formations around and about the body. In elaborate sequences of moves, the hoops are made to interlock, and in such a way they can be extended from the body of the dancer to form appendages such as wings and tails. The hoops are handmade by the dancers out of simple plastic piping and wrapped in colorful tapes.

Another Native American dance is the Shawl Dance, or the Fancy Shawl Dance, which is a traditional woman's dance.

Women's fancy shawl dancers wear beaded capes, moccasins and leggings and most importantly, a beautifully decorated long fringed shawl. Their colorful outfits evoke images of beautiful butterflies when they are dancing. The origin of Women's Fancy Dance is relatively recent on the powwow trail. It was originally danced in the northern part of Indian country by a few brave women, who were sometimes booed for their efforts by people who felt that women should not call such attention to their dancing. Women's fancy dance features fancy footwork, a very fast pace and brightly colored shawls worn draped over the shoulders. Fancy shawl dancers have adapted many newer materials in their regalia such as cut glass beads, rhinestones, sequins, ribbon, and fabric.

Corresponding to the Women's Fancy Shawl Dance, the men have their version: The Men's Fancy Dance.

One of the more interesting dances in the Pow wow, Men's Fancy dance is the most strenuous and athletic. To be good at this dance, the dancer must train for stamina and agility. The dance is fast and features jumps and twirling. The regalia is said to represent the rainbow spirits in its bright colors and flying feathers and ribbons. The Men's Fancy dancer typically wears two bustles of bright colored feathers with added ribbon, feather or horse hair hackles and bright arm and head bands repeating the colors and patterns. The dancer also wears a headdress roach trimmed in colored horsehair and featuring two eagle feathers. The roach is designed to keep the feathers either spinning or rocking in movement. It is part of the dance to keep the feathers moving constantly throughout the song. Dancers also carry coup sticks which are highly decorated with ribbons or feathers. The coup stick was originally a small stick carried into battle by a warrior. It was considered a great sign of bravery if you were able to touch your enemy with your coup stick (much more brave than killing your enemy).

Another dance that highlights Native American women is the Jingle Dance.

The Jingle Dance (Sometimes called the Jingle Dress Dance)

The Jingle Dance, according to modern records, has its origins with the Ojibwe people. As the story goes, a medicine man's granddaughter was very ill. He had a dream in which a spirit wearing the jingle dress came to him and told him to make one of these dresses and put it on his daughter to cure her. When he awoke, he and his wife proceeded to assemble the dress as described by the spirit of his dream. When finished, they and others brought his granddaughter to the dance hall and she put on the dress. During the first circle around the room, she needed to be carried. During the second circle around the room, she could barely walk and needed the assistance of several women. The third circle around the room she found she could walk without assistance and during the fourth circle around the room, she danced. The jingle dress is made of a cloth, velvet or leather base adorned with jingles made out of a shiny metal. Traditionally and still common today, the jingles are made from the lids of snuff cans. These are bent and molded into triangular bell shapes and attached to the dress with ribbon or fabric in a pattern designed by the dancer. It takes between 400 and 700 jingles to make an adult jingle dress. Different customs dictate the number of jingles and some dresses have one jingle for each day.

The dance itself is designed to incorporate the sound of the jingles by allowing them to move; that is, to make them jingle, or be made "happy." The steps are controlled and do not involve high kicking or twirls. Often the steps are in a zig-zag pattern to reflect the zigzagging involved in the journey of life. Similar to Men's Grass dancing, the feet often do parallel movements. Similar to a Women's Traditional dancer, the Jingle Dress dancer also raises her fan when the "honor beats" are played on the d rum. As in all dances, the Jingle Dress dancer must stay in time with the drum beat and stop with both feet on the ground on the final beat.

The Round Dance

One of the more popular of the Native American dances is the Round Dance or The Friendship Dance. Native American round dance is not anything like ballroom dancing, however, it is a dance that has long been held as a courting activity. It is performed during the inter-tribal social portion of a powwow as well as on many social occasions. The round dance has an infectious upbeat tempo and creates a simple and fun activity. The dance consist some easy-to-follow moves which are performed while dancing in a circle

The origins of Round Dance come from the healing dances of the Plains Indians – it retains its spiritual core and inspires joy and happiness – men and women, young and old dance in a spectacular display of kinship and harmony. This dance is one of the few Native American dances in which women get to dance with men. Native American traditional dances are usually segregated by gender. The Round Dance is also a popular dance for non-Indians during an inter-tribal gathering. It is an easy dance to follow as everyone joins hands inside the sacred circle forming a big circle moving clockwise, or without joining hands they move clockwise stepping to the beat of the drum. If there are many people participating, than a second circle is formed inside the first circle that moves in the opposite direction. The Round dance creates a simple and fun activity that brings both cultures together for positive interaction. In the recent past, this social dance music has gained in popularity among the Native American community and is moving into the mainstream as a popular music style. Native American dance is centered around the drum, so it makes sense that drums are a crucial part of Round Dance music...the only difference is the size of the drum. Rather than of the deep, thunderous sounds of the larger pedestal drums typically associated with native song, Round Dance music among many tribes often features the spirited sounds of the much smaller single headed hand drum – whether performed by one singer or a large group of singers, each beats a drum while singing – each song features soaring vocals set to the steady, resonating beat of the drum. We Nuluti Equani Ehi does not use the smaller drums, by preference staying with the large, deep-voiced drum. The Round Dance was mainly performed in the winter time. Although these social dances can take place during a powwow, they can also be experienced as a singular event…some of these indoor winter gatherings have been known to last throughout the night, often finishing after sunrise.

Another of the welll-known dances is the men's Duck and Dive.

The Duck and Dive Dance

Other Dances

There are many other dances that may or may not be performed, depending on the dancers who attend the Pow Wow. Among those are the Chicken Dance, the Butterfly Dance, the Candy Dance (reserved for the children who, when the drum pauses, gather up candy that has been spread on the ground), Men's and Women's Traditional Dance, the Sun Dance and other dances that are performed by different tribes.

Finale.

As the Pow wow comes to an end, the Eagle Staff bearer and the flag bearers re-enter the sacred circle, secure their flags and march out to the beat of the drum. Once the flags have been secured, the Pow wow Arena Director informs the attendants that the final song is being sung and everyone is welcome to gather around the drum for the finale.

Postscript

To our brothers and sisters of all races and all tribes: Greetings!

The Nuluti Equani Ehi Tribe does not wish to challenge the Cherokee, the Cree, the Ojibwe, the Iroquois, the Apache or any other tribe, nation or band in their bloodlines as we are **all** descendents from the First Nations, the people that migrated to the Americas from other areas, primarily Siberia, and established all current existing tribes numbering in the thousands. After all, we—and all other Native Americans—are **Anishinaabe People,** the Original Man, created by the breath of the God of Life – *Gichi-Manidoo* – which many of our brothers call the Great Spirit.

We, the Nuluti Equani Ehi, are of **Anishinaabe Algonquin** blood as are many of our blood kin: the Cherokee, the Cree, the Catawba, the Delaware, the Sioux, the Lakota, The Apache, the Navajo, the Puma and countless other tribes. As such, our bloodlines cross the bloodlines of many other tribes as intermingling of bloodlines has occurred for thousands of years. Additionally, inter-relations between races resulted in our sharing blood with whites, blacks, tans, yellows of all sorts. We are still each a member of that ethnic class referred to as "Native American." This label is false in that we are all migratory and came to the Americas from other lands so long ago that it is lost in history. None the less, the title of "Native American" is certainly no insult, rather it is an honor; an honor that we share with many of our brothers in blood.

The Nuluti Equani Ehi Tribe has not sought federal recognition as it has not been needed or wanted. We are not at this time federally recognized by the B.I.A and we may well choose to remain without seeking recognition, as we find the intrusion of the government into tribal teachings and customs to be reprehensible and intrusive. It is the custom among our people to obtain what is needed for our people through our own work and with assistance from those others who agree with our mission. Rather than excluding any, we welcome blood-brothers and blood-sisters of all tribes who wish to join with us. And we invite our brothers and sisters from all nations to visit with us and learn our ways. Welcome all.

Taku waste econ, ka ituya yani kte sni

Chief Jim Wilson